*Clive Barda* is internationally recognised as one of this country's leading photographers of the performing arts; his work is in the permanent collections of the National Portrait Gallery and the National Museum of Photography. He first visited the Festival in 1979, and in 1993 he began a three year project photographing visiting artists at work, capturing not only the emotional intensity that so many performers bring to their art, but also some of the more offbeat aspects of Edinburgh in August. Added to work selected from his archive of 25 years, his images offer a fascinating contrast to those of the earlier years.

*Paul Shillabeer's* unique contribution to this book stems from his photographic record of every Festival from the very first in 1947 until 1973. He captured not just the stage highlights of that era, but the remarkable number of social events the Festival spawned in its wake. This is the first time his pictures have been made available to the general public and the Festival acknowledges the generosity of his family in allowing their publication.

*Sean Hudson's* ability to record both performers and productions in a memorable way has brought him successive commissions from Festival managements over the years. The quality of his work has never been more apparent than in the photographs reproduced in this celebratory book.

*Alex "Tug" Wilson's* pictures demonstrate one of the other little heralded skills necessary to good Festival photography... the ability to make three hundred dashes from theatre rehearsal to photo call to performance without running out of steam, film or inspiration.

*Ruth Wishart* is a Scottish journalist and broadcaster with a long standing interest in the arts who writes a weekly column, presents a daily radio programme, and trains every August as one of the Festival's resident groupies.

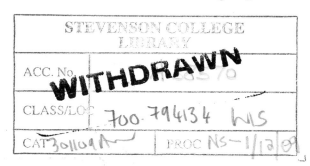

EDINBURGH
INTERNATIONAL
FESTIVAL

50 YEARS IN
PHOTOGRAPHS

Written by

Ruth Wishart

sponsored by

The Royal Bank
of Scotland

Published by the **Edinburgh Festival Society**
21 Market Street,
Edinburgh EH1 1BW.
Registered Charity Nº: SC004694

ISBN  0 903605 07 4

Designed and produced by **Oxygen,** London and Edinburgh.
Printed in Great Britain by **Jackson Wilson Limited,** Leeds.

Printed on Mohawk Superfine Original White Eggshell paper supplied at a specially discounted price by **Paper Resources Limited,** Oxfordshire. Thanks also to Bookbridge (a division of Woodland International) Brentwood, for help with freight costs.

(1) Frontispiece: Fireworks Finale **1950**.

Edinburgh Festival...

## contents

*(2) Benjamin Britten's **Death in Venice**, Scottish Opera 1983.*

"*We wish to provide the world with a centre where, year after year, all that is best in music and drama and the visual arts can be seen and heard in ideal surroundings.*"

*Sir John Falconer, Lord Provost of Edinburgh 1947.*

*lovely evening - can we NOT do it again?*

There have been imitations – always flattering. And there are other festivals principally devoted to music or drama which have spanned decades, survived critics, and deservedly become the stuff of legend.

But the Edinburgh International Festival, grown organically in Scotland's capital city from the unpromising and supposedly infertile soil of the immediate post war period, has truly earned the term unique. In the fifty years since that opening concert in the summer of 1947 it has hosted all the world's principal orchestras and soloists, occasioned operatic triumphs, produced memorable international drama, attracted extraordinary choreography, lured the major directorial talents of two generations and given birth to some truly stunning exhibitions. It has also been great fun!

Because Edinburgh in August obeys the first law of festivals… above all else to provide a celebration. The celebrants have the enviable bonus of a Festival city with a discernible heart. Nobody can come to this city in that month without being touched in some way by the sheer exuberance and colossal variety of its cultural menu, and the tangible sense of excitement in its historic streets and public squares. If its citizenry have sometimes looked askance at the accompanying invasion of the amalgamated union of unicyclists, fire-eaters, jugglers and strolling players, they have also nursed – in a suitably douce and understated fashion – a deep pride in the prestige the Festival enjoys. The following pages are not a history of that Festival; other publications will provide that with a proper concern for chronology and detail. What this book offers is an incomparable glimpse of the performers, backstage as well as front; and a flavour of just some of the superb highlights as caught by the lenses of Festival photographers over five decades.

Many of these pictures have never been seen before. They have never been the subject of collective appraisal until now. The most difficult task of all has been to discard several thousand images in the effort to provide a balanced flavour across the art forms. They say that a good picture is worth a thousand words. These snapshots of forty-nine Festivals will also evoke a thousand memories; recall the emotion, the laughter, and those moments when the hair on the back of your neck informs you that you have been privileged to be present at an unforgettable performance.

*(3) Opposite: Hebbel Theater's mesmeric **Dr Faustus Lights the Lights** directed by **Robert Wilson** in 1993.*

3

# Music *and* Maestros

*(4) Above: **Arthur Oldham** and **Richard Armstrong** rehearse*

***Moses and Aaron** for the 1992 opening concert.*

*(5) Opposite: **Sir Thomas Beecham** in Havana mode.*

*1948* - one year after the inaugural Edinburgh Festival and Sir Thomas Beecham, then conducting the Scottish Orchestra, had no doubts: "The people of Scotland are damned fools to throw away £60,000 on a music festival."

Of course at that juncture our Tommy wasn't exactly a neutral, given that he was anxious for funds for his own band. But by the following year, like most early sceptics, he had been firmly recruited to the ranks of the true believers.

The next year he was in charge of the opening concert with the Royal Philharmonic under his baton. And, like most of the world's great conductors, he forged a long lasting relationship with the Festival, in his case finishing with a tenth anniversary concert where patrons found themselves with both Beecham and Sir Arthur Bliss.

If theatrical highlights are often encapsulated by a stunning piece of visual imagery, the musical equivalents are frequently characterised by raw emotion.

*(6) Bruno Walter and Kathleen Ferrier entrance the*
*first Festival in 1947.*

Some special combination of circumstances leaves audiences aware that their collective experience will continue to produce the most exquisite kind of retrospective pleasure.

For many that recognition came in year one, when Bruno Walter was reunited with the Vienna Philharmonic for the first time since the outbreak of World War Two.

Some of his colleagues had not survived the attentions of the Nazis. But the orchestra was the rigorous machine of old and their decision to come to Edinburgh in 1947 could not have given a firmer stamp of intended excellence to the venture.

But there was another relationship forged that year which has passed into musical history. Kathleen Ferrier appeared with the orchestra in Mahler's *Song of the Earth* in an unforgettable performance.

She was destined to have too few return engagements in Edinburgh, though her 1952 performance with Sir John Barbirolli's Hallé Orchestra in Elgar's *Dream of Gerontius*, her last before her death a year later, also challenged the critics' grasp of superlatives.

Barbirolli payed tribute to that talent, and that loss, in a 1954 Verdi *Requiem* with the Hallé and the Sheffield Philharmonic Chorus, signalling to the audience to rise as the final notes died away. Another night of heart-stopping emotion.

But then he was a conductor with an unerring eye for the theatrical as he proved with his candlelit performance of Haydn's *Farewell Symphony* at the Usher Hall in 1966. When he died in 1970 he had been a popular fixture in 11 separate programmes and should have conducted the first of the bicentennial Beethoven concerts that year.

As it transpired 1970 was still memorable for a host of reasons, not least the stamina and commitment of Arthur Oldham's Edinburgh Festival Chorus who opened that year in Beethoven's *Ninth Symphony* with Colin Davis and the New Philharmonia, closed the proceedings with Beethoven's *Choral Fantasy for Piano and Chorus*

*(7) Yehudi Menuhin adds sartorial sparkle to an Usher Hall rehearsal.*

with the SNO and Sir Alexander Gibson, and also found time to rehearse and perform the *Missa Solemnis* with Carlo Maria Giulini and the New Philharmonia.

That neither Oldham nor his charges have lost their touch over the years was apparent in the 1992 opening concert as they tackled the might of *Moses and Aaron* and emerged well ahead on points.

The musical cast list of the Edinburgh Festival and a history of great orchestral moments and major conducting talents in the second half of the Twentieth Century are well nigh interchangeable. All the great orchestras from France, Germany, Italy, Holland,

Spain and Austria have made pilgrimages to the Edinburgh shrine.

Russia and Czechoslovakia led the charge from Eastern Europe whilst the orchestras of Boston, Chicago, Pittsburgh and Cleveland followed the pioneering example of the New York Philharmonic in 1951 in adding the cream of the new world.

In those days the Atlantic was crossed by the more leisurely sea route, so there was no question of doing a mere Festival concert. A season was both the lure and the minimum requirement.

Subsequently other fine orchestras have taken week long residencies including Pittsburgh and Simon Rattle's City of Birmingham Symphony while the Scottish National Orchestra and the BBC Scottish Symphony Orchestra regularly work overtime.

Meanwhile, over the years, and often in the same year, the rostrum has been mounted by a Who's Who of the orchestral greats. Von Karajan, Wand and Klemperer. Giulini, Muti, Masur, Haitink and Tennstedt. Rattle, Previn, Boulez and Abbado. Menuhin, Bernstein, Ozawa and Jansons. Ashkenazy, Lazarev and Temirkanov. Solti, Stokowski, Gibson and Davis. Barbirolli, Beecham, Mackerras, Furtwängler and Walter.

Occasionally the emotion was fuelled not just by the participants but by outside events. In 1968 pickets greeted the arrival of the State Orchestra of the USSR in protest at the invasion of Czechoslovakia.

Yet during their performance, the players and the audience forged a warm understanding of that orchestra's sensitive dilemma. At that same Festival Yehudi Menuhin, who normally let his instrument provide his eloquence, felt moved to precede his performance of Beethoven's *Violin Concerto* by announcing that: "I dedicate this programme, as Beethoven did his life, to the indomitable and defiant spirit of man."

A reprise of a sort came in 1991 with another visit of the Leningrad Philharmonic. They had left home before the tanks rolled into Moscow, and arrived in Edinburgh not knowing when or even whether they could return home. Or what they would find there when they did.

That uncertainty somehow unleashed a new passion in their playing and everyone present knew they had heard an utterly compelling performance.

The Usher Hall hasn't produced all the Festival's musical fireworks. In morning recitals at the Freemasons' and Queen's Halls, in late night performances at the Lyceum, in all manner of implausible venues, soloists and ensembles have also left indelible marks on the Festival programmes.

Consummate performances from John Ogdon, Clifford Curzon, Peter Donohoe, Richard Goode, Artur Schnabel, Alfred Brendel. A tradition of operatic excellence translating into individual recitals by Felicity Lott, Jessye Norman, Barbara Hendricks, Victoria de Los Angeles, Galina Gorchakova, Dietrich Fischer-Dieskau and countless others.

Masterly showcases by the Amadeus, Hungarian, Borodin, Shostakovich and Melos quartets and many more.

Virtuoso displays from Julian Bream, Mstislav Rostropovich, Ravi Shankar, Isaac Stern, András Schiff and Jacqueline du Pré.

In some cases the performers made common cause not just with the Festival audiences, but with the wider Scottish community. 1958 found Menuhin with pianist Louis Kentner and cellist Gaspard Cassado giving a concert at a cinema in a peripheral Edinburgh housing scheme.

They were uncertain of their likely reception and thrilled to find the building queued round the block. It set an agreeable precedent which found members of the Glyndebourne and Czech operas giving similar extra-mural performances in Leith while Isaac Stern entranced the denizens of Portobello.

Meanwhile Peter Maxwell Davis, some 25 years later, proved that off-beat venues can attract new fans when he brought huge numbers of young people into his concerts at Haymarket Ice Rink. It is not recorded if the orchestra demanded cold weather payments.

*(8) Opposite: **Jacqueline du Pré** - in Edinburgh at the height of her very special powers.*

*(9) Opposite above: Intensity from any angle -* **John Ogdon**
*at the Usher Hall in* **1965**.

*(10) Opposite below:* **Alfred Brendel** *- a study in concentration.*

*(11) Above:* **Artur Rubinstein** *in full flight in* **1954**.

*(12) Opposite:* **Richard Goode** *captures*
*The Queen's Hall in* **1994**.
*(13) Above:* **Alicia de Larrocha** *at the same*
*venue in* **1995**.
*(14) Left:* **Peter Donohoe** *learns that lunch is*
*at hand in* **1992**.

*(15) **Andrés Segovia** - a memorable soloist in **1948**.*

*(16)* **Ravi Shankar** *adding the splendour of the Orient in* **1971**.

*Age shall not wither them - but conductors are not entirely unscathed.*
*(17)* **Sir John Barbirolli** *as a young maestro in* **1949** *and (18) opposite*
*rather later that same century.*

*(19)* **Sir Alexander Gibson** *working on the Festival debut*
*of his beloved Scottish Opera in* **1967***.*

*(20) And they wowed them at the movies too -*
**Menuhin, Cassado** *and* **Kentner** *take the Festival*
*to a cinema in the local housing estates in* **1958.**

*Batons, grins, threats and hand signals - all part of the conductor's arsenal!*

*Clockwise from top left: (21)* **John Eliot Gardiner**, *(22)* **Kurt Masur**, *(23)* **Richard Armstrong**, *(24)* **Charles Mackerras** *and (25)* **Sándor Végh**.

*Clockwise from top left:*
*(26)* **Pierre Boulez,**
*(27)* **André Previn,** *and youthful*
*appearances by*
*(28)* **Lorin Maazel** *and*
*(29)* **Carlo Maria Giulini.**

*The gentle art of producing pianissimo:*

*(30) Above:* **Sir Georg Solti**.

*(31) Opposite:* **Bernard Haitink**.

(32) Opposite: **Herbert von Karajan**
*rehearses 'The Boys from Berlin' in **1967**.*
(33) *Above:* **Mariss Jansons.**
(34) *Right:* **Otto Klemperer in 1961.**

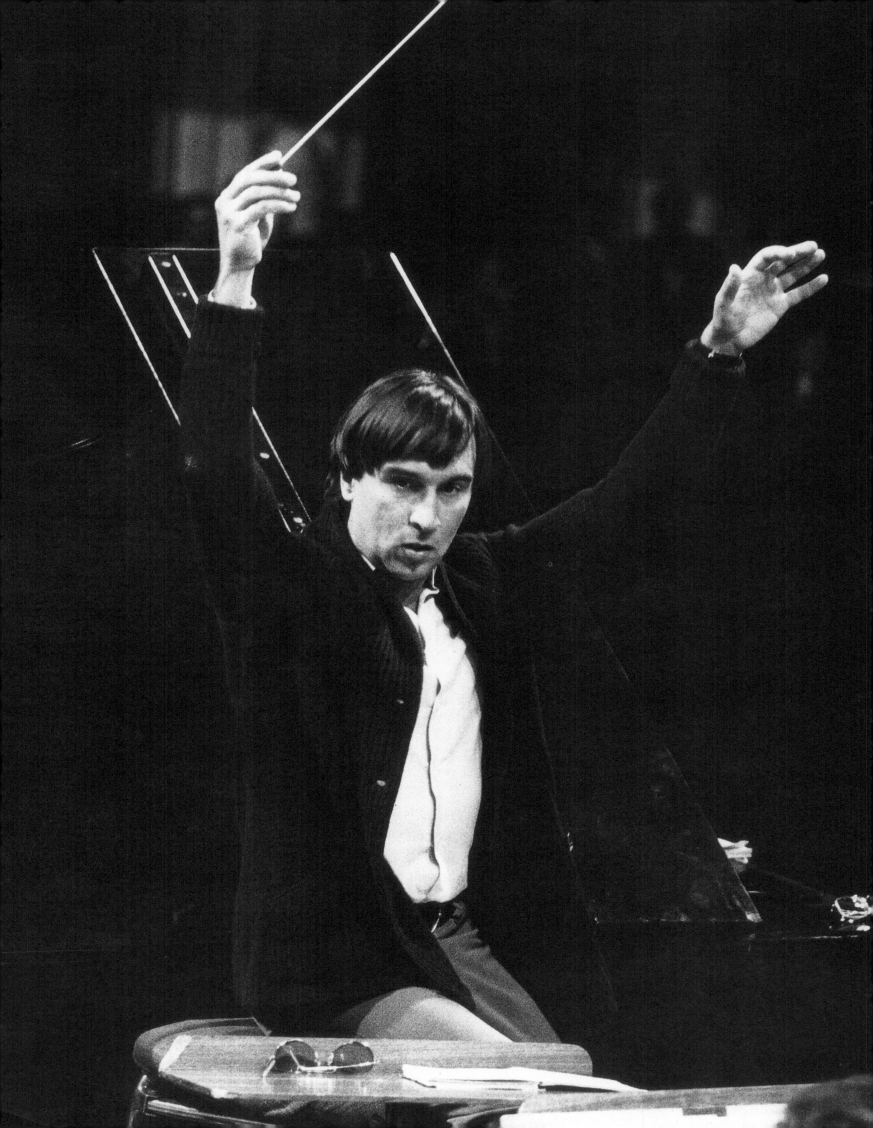

*(35) Opposite: **I Claudio!
Abbado** reaches for perfection.
(36) Above: Celebration concert
marking the farewell to
**Peter Diamand,** with
**Claudio Abbado, Daniel Barenboim**
and **Isaac Stern, 1978.**
(37) Left: **The Amadeus String
Quartet** with **Gervase de Peyer**
in 1959.*

*(38)* **The Ladies Band** *from 1991 - The Open Theatre of Belgrade with the Jean Anouilh play concerning an all female orchestra's less musical moments.*

(39) *Above:* **Ron Berglas,**
**The Double Bass, 1990.**
(40) *Right: Double basses await their*
*Usher Hall entrance.*

(41) *Above:* **The Edinburgh Festival Chorus**
*on stage and (42) right, in rehearsal, **1993**.*

*(43)* **Fireworks Concert** *crowds on Princes Street in* **1994**.

*(44) **Wolfgang Holzmair** and **Gerard Wyss**
in rehearsal in **1995.***

(45) Above: **Peter Schreier** and **András Schiff**
in **1995**.

(46) Right: **Thomas Quasthoff, 1993**.

(47) Far right: **Anne Sofie von Otter** and
**Alastair Miles** break from Usher Hall rehearsals.

# NIGHT *Owls*

They called it *Beyond the Fringe.* And in fact the debut of Jonathan Miller, Dudley Moore, Alan Bennett and Peter Cook was an official Festival event in 1960. Daring stuff it was too by the standards of these pre-satirical times. The most risky precedent after all had been Flanders and Swann the year before. Delightful of course but not perhaps at the cutting edge!

Over the years the Festival hasn't gone in for a massive amount of what we might call cabaret, but when it does indulge it has generally got it right. 1965 brought a teutonic pout swiftly followed by the rest of Marlene Dietrich. The sultry one was a riotous success with everyone, bar the Festival office's redoubtable Ellen Valentine.

The latter stalwart worked for six Festival directors in some capacity before her recent retirement, and was underwhelmed by Ms Dietrich's imperious demand for a stack of headed Festival notepaper. Ellen wasn't at all sure what she wanted to do with it. But she wasn't going to risk finding out. The megastar got a polite but firm "nein".
Ellen one, Marlene nil.

Sultry in a different way was M. Charles Aznavour, who contrived to inject a remarkable amount of sex appeal into a small slim body in 1967. And that year also saw one of several visits from his compatriot Marcel Marceau a man for whom mime seems an inadequate description for such lavish talents.

Under the "now for something completely different" category came Max Wall's *Buster* in 1977 while audiences are still recovering from the sight of Cleo Laine almost subsumed by an all-tartan supporting cast in '87.

*(48) Left: The Fab Four Pre-Beatles **Jonathan Miller**, **Dudley Moore, Alan Bennett and Peter Cook** get Beyond the Fringe in 1960.*

*(49) Top left: **Juliette Greco** in 1961.*

*(50) Top right: **Robert Ponsonby** - Godfather of Festival cabaret.*

*(51) Above: **The Flying Karamazov Brothers** - not brothers, not Russian, and they don't fly - in 1990.*

*(52) Opposite left: **Flanders** and **Swann** on song in 1959.*

(53) Above: **ssshharles Aznavour 1967**.

*The other sound of the sixties.*

(54) Opposite: **La Dietrich** *smoulders in '65.*

*(55) Hoots! It's **Cleo** in 1987.*

*(56) **Max Wall** starred with **Jan Waters** in a short musical based on **Buster Keaton** in a 1977 late night offering.*

(57) Above: **Marceau** the man and
(58) opposite: the mime in **1967**.

# All *the* World's our Stage

(59) *Above:* **Rikki Fulton** *and* **Paul Young** *in*
**A Wee Touch of Class** *- freely translated by Denise Coffey from*
*Le Bourgeois Gentilhomme in 1986.*

(60) *Opposite:* **Alan Rickman** *in* **Tango at the End of Winter**
*directed by* **Yukio Ninagawa** *in 1991.*

That the annual Arts Festival in Edinburgh was entitled to insert the word International was never in doubt from the earliest days. Alongside the Old Vic Company's *the Taming of The Shrew*, and *Richard II* in 1947 – the latter produced by Ralph Richardson and starring Alec Guinness – came the Louis Jouvet company with *L'Ecole des Femmes* and *Ondine*. The message was clear: the Festival would pitch for excellence in whatever country they located it, and have it performed in whichever language was appropriate. Which didn't preclude the taking of some very entertaining liberties.

Another version of *L'Ecole*, adapted for a 1961 production by Robert Kemp, emerged in broad Scots retitled *Let Wives Tak Tent* (Take Care). Starring the magnificently lugubrious Duncan Macrae, it was an early indication of an under-explored side of the Auld

Alliance between Scotland and France – how French playwrights like Molière could find a natural rhythm in the Scots tongue without losing humour or subtlety. And over the years that proposition has held good with Franco-Scottish versions of *Tartuffe*, *Le Misanthrope* and *Le Bourgeois Gentilhomme* among others.

Those early years set a pattern where major figures in UK drama came to Edinburgh but featured in programmes which also included both established foreign companies and those who used the Festival as a launching pad for later celebrity. Frank Dunlop, who came to the Festival in the 80s with a reputation for innovative drama through his work with Pop Theatre and the Young Vic, was always enthusiastic about springing surprises on his audiences, he says, rather

than only "buying established goods off the shelf".

One of those shocks – in the most satisfactory possible way – was the arrival of a Japanese company, then called Toho, under the direction of Yukio Ninagawa in 1985. Over the five decades of the Festival there have been many memorable interpretations of "The Scottish Play": Ann Todd's Lady Macbeth with the Old Vic in 1954, a Kunju production in 1987 as part of the Chinese theatre season and the somewhat notorious Bremer Theater version two years later. But that Toho *Macbeth*, with its central images of Buddha and the Cherry Blossom forest, set Edinburgh alight and began a love affair between Ninagawa and the Festival audiences which lasted many years. He was to come back with a series of extraordinary productions including *The Tempest*. But sometimes a pervasive theatrical memory hinges on just one image. And it was the Ninagawa *Medea*, performed outdoors in the old quadrangle of Edinburgh University, which produced one of the most unforgettable moments in five decades with its finale – a shining chariot flying upwards over the university rooftops.

Occasionally the civic authorities got a mite nervous about such seminal moments. 1969 was dominated, by common consent, by Ian McKellen's mesmerising *Edward II* which he played in repertoire with *Richard II* at the Assembly Hall. You will recall that Edward meets a rather unsavoury end which gives a whole new meaning to the phrase anally retentive.

Some of the local councillors felt the scene in question liable to upset and offend the lieges. Fortunately the press officer was blessed with inspiration at precisely the right moment. He invited the Moderator of the General Assembly of the Church of Scotland to a rehearsal. The Moderator pronounced himself both impressed and unfazed. And, since Moderators outrank mere councillors by several pips in Scotland's capital, the controversy was stillborn.

McKellen appeared that year with Prospect Theatre directed by Toby Robertson, another company with a long and fruitful relationship with the Festival. Timothy West's *Lear* and his *Dr Johnson* with Prospect also proved outstanding moments in their Festival history.

In other years McKellen appeared with the RSC and was involved in the birth of The Actors' Company, a creation so determinedly democratic that his first role with them was a pageboy. The fact that the Festival gave this glittery but untested group their first major showcase encouraged several visits.

Though within a very few years of its launch, the Festival had little difficulty in persuading both major stars and world renowned companies to appear in what was already recognised as a uniquely prestigious event.

A glance through the theatre credits finds startlingly different Hamlets from Richard Burton and Tom Courteney, a much acclaimed Pericles from Derek Jacobi, the novelty of the Mystery Plays on tour indoors and out with Brian Glover as God, and endless innovation from Dunlop's Young Vic with Denise Coffey in a somewhat free adaptation of *The Comedy of Errors*. And the same company, including Edward Fox, in *Bible One*, the second part of which featured a glorious romp with music by some young hopeful called Lloyd Webber. *Joseph and the Amazing Technicolour Dreamcoat* was staged at the then Haymarket Ice Rink, one of many unlikely venues pressed into service as the Festival perfected its Topsy impersonation.

The theatrical grandes dames sojourned north to this startling new event as well. Dame Sybil Thorndike reciting at St Cecilia's, Dame Edith Evans at the Lyceum, the incomparable Dame Peggy Ashcroft, girlish in *Aspects of Women* in 1958 and effortlessly assured in Lillian Hellman's *Watch on the Rhine* in 1980. Margaret Lockwood as Eliza in *Pygmalion*, Claire Bloom as both Ophelia and Juliet and fine performances from Tutin and Dench. Sometimes too the quirkiness of the casting added that indefinable ingredient which separates the memorable from the competent, like a 1966 *Trojan Women* with Flora Robson playing alongside Jane Asher and Cleo Laine.

*(61) Top:* **Medea** *- staged outdoors in the university quadrangle in* **1986.** *Even when the heavens opened, the audience refused to leave.*

*(62) Above: A scene from* **The Tempest** *in* **1988.**

*(63) Right:* **Yukio Ninagawa** *and his company had a rich relationship with the Festival in the 1980s.*

Speak to those Festival recidivists whose attendance spans many of these five decades and all will produce personal favourites: Elsa Vergi's *Medea* with the Piraiklon Theatre Company in 1966; Gielgud's 1948 production of the same play. The visit of Tadeuz Kantor's Cricot 2 company from Krakow in 1980; the Romanian *Ubu Rex* in 1991; James Baldwin's *Amen Corner* in 1965; an intensely moving *Miss Julie* with the African actor John Kani; *Poppy Nongena* from New York; Ekkehard Schall with the Berliner Ensemble, and countless other individual pieces of theatrical magic. But some productions have so impinged themselves on the collective consciousness that they have carved themselves a special niche in Edinburgh's hall of dramatic fame.

When Teatro Libero arrived from Italy in 1970 few people outside of Festival Director Peter Diamand knew what to expect of *Orlando Furioso*. In fact this joyous and anarchic performance, based on a narrative poem by Ludovico Ariosto, challenged all preconceptions of the relationship between cast and audience. The latter, involuntarily cast as strolling players, found themselves amidst glorious mayhem and indeed in the flightpath of alarmingly realistic giant horses on wheels. It was a raging success and one of the great triumphs of the story so far.

Inevitably, with a lifespan of half a century, many directors have been unable to resist the temptation to re-interpret previous productions. Shakespeare, Shaw,

*(64) **Orlando Furioso** changed the face of Festival drama in 1970.*

Schiller, Ibsen, and Brecht re-emerge at regular intervals whilst the body count in successive Greek tragedies represents truly impressive stage carnage.

But one play has found itself inextricably interwoven with the fabric of the Edinburgh Festival.

*Ane Satyre of the Thrie Estaites* was written by Sir David Lyndsay in 1540. Its last known public outing prior to the Festival was in 1552. It's an unconscionable time for a playwright to await a revival, but let's hope Sir David found posthumous pleasure in the production which was launched in 1948.

*(65) **Dame Sensuality** - so good they named her twice! This production opened in 1984 and had 12 more performances in 1985.*

Nurtured by James Bridie, adapted by Robert Kemp and produced by Tyrone Guthrie, nobody could gainsay the pedigree. Neither was that first cast exactly anonymous.

Kemp had wanted the production to appeal to many Scots who might have sought employment in the south. He seems to have succeeded with a cast which included Duncan Macrae, Stanley Baxter, Robert Urquhart, Bryden Murdoch, Moultrie Kelsall, Lennox Milne and Jean Taylor Smith.

By 1973 the Festival was on it's 5th *Estaite*, and still attracting the major Scottish talents – among that year's lineup, John Cairney, John Grieve and Rikki Fulton. But one of its best outings was in '84 with the late Andrew Cruickshank cheerfully leering at Dame Sensuality from beneath his clerical headgear.

Then, in 1996, John McGrath upped the ante with *The Four Estaites* - the Lords Spiritual in Westminster, the Lords Temporal in Brussels, the Multinational Corporate Merchants and the Media Moguls.

Yet in the decade approaching the Millennium the Festival can hardly be accused of settling for cosy familiarity. Brian McMaster, the latest director to be let loose in this wondrous toyshop, has forged important relationships with those whose work is at the cutting edge of european and world drama.

His tenure has brought us Peter Stein's ambitious *Julius Caesar*, Luc Bondy's *The Hour We Knew Nothing of Each Other*, Robert Wilson's staging of Gertrude Stein's *Dr Faustus Lights the Lights*, Robert Lepage's *Seven Streams of the River Ota*, and a succession of typically adventurous works from Peter Sellars.

1996 brought Lepage back with his idiosyncratic solo Hamlet, *Elsinore*, while Robert Wilson returned to the work of Gertrude Stein with Houston Grand Opera's *Four Saints in Three Acts*.

To maintain its enviable reputation Edinburgh constantly needs to attract such talents. But it can take some satisfaction from the number of these innovators who now consider the Edinburgh Festival an unmissable destination for their work.

*(66)* **Ian McKellen's Richard II** *and* **Edward II in 1969** *remain memorable highlights of five decades of international drama.*

*(67) **Bryden Murdoch** at his most regal in **1948**.*

(68) *Top left:* **The Thrie Estaites 1959** *with* **James Gibson, Walter Carr** *and* **Duncan Macrae.**

(69) *Bottom left:* **Andrew Cruickshank** *goes clerical in* **1984.**

(70) *Below:* **1973 Estaites:**
**Rikki Fulton, John Grieve** *and*
**John Cairney.**

(71) *Opposite:* **Sir Tyrone Guthrie** *revived* **The Thrie Estaites** *in* **1948.**

*(72) Above:* **Tom Courteney's** *controversial* **Hamlet** *in 1968.*

*(73) Opposite:* **Alfred Marks** *celebrates his appointment to the RSC!*
*Marks played Falstaff in their* **1980** *production of* **Henry IV Part 2**.

*(74) **Richard Burton** and **Fay Compton** in The Old Vic **Hamlet** in 1953.*

*(75)* **Eva Mattes** *in Berliner Ensemble's* **Antony & Cleopatra,** *1994.*

*(76)* **Derek Jacobi** *as Pericles and* **Marilyn Taylerson** *as Marina in 1973.*

*Clockwise from top left: (77) Toho **Macbeth**, 1985,
(78) Kunju **Macbeth**, 1987, (79) Traverse **Macbeth**, 1965,
(80) Bremer **Macbeth**, 1989.*

*(81) Edinburgh Festival Productions' version of **The Tempest** in 1978.*

*(82 & 83) Frank Dunlop's Pop Theatre with*
***A Midsummer Night's Dream** in 1967.* **Robin Bailey**
*and* **Cleo Laine** *were Oberon and Titania,*
**Hywel Bennett** *was Puck and* **Jim Dale** *played Bottom.*

(84) Opposite: *Bless you my audience.*
**Brian Glover** *as God in the National Theatre Company's*
**The Passion** *in 1980.*

(85) Above right: **Bible One**, *The Young Vic, 1972.*

(86) Right: **William Dudley's** *original sketch*
*for* **The Bakers' Play**.

(87) Above: **The Bakers' Play** *unfolds*
*in Parliament Square.*

(88) *Above:* **Edwige Feuillère** *brought her own company to*
*Edinburgh with* **La Dame aux Camélias** *in 1955.*
(89) *Opposite:* **Peggy Ashcroft** *in* **Aspects of Women:**
**From Chaucer to Dylan Thomas** *in 1958.*

*(90) Left:* **Judi Dench** *impossibly*
*youthful with The Old Vic's*
**The Double Dealer** *in 1959.*
*(91) Above:* **Maggie Smith** *and* **John**
**Justin** *in* **The Double Dealer** *in 1959.*
*Opposite: No Dames More Grandes!*
*(92)* **Sybil Thorndike** *in 1969,*
*(93)* **Edith Evans** *in 1984,*
*(94)* **Claire Bloom** *in* **These Are**
**Women (1983)**
*and (95)* **Dorothy Tutin**
*and* **Max Adrian** *in* **The Devils**
*with the RSC in 1962.*

(96) *Above,* (97) *left and*
(98) *top left:* **The Trojan Women** *as conceived by Pop Theatre in* **1966** *with* **Cleo Laine, Jane Asher** *and* **Flora Robson.**
(99) *Bottom left: La Mama's* **Trojan Women, 1976,** *with* **Valois Mickens.**

*(100)* **Honor Blackman**, *sans leather, as Yvette -* **The Life and Times of Yvette Guilbert** *in 1990.*

(101) *Opposite:* **Joan Littlewood** *surveys the Assembly Hall in* **1964***.*

(102) *Above:* **Felicity Kendal** *in the National Theatre's* **On the Razzle***,* **1981***.*

*(103 & 104) The Abbey Theatre's*
**Playboy of the Western World, 1968.**

(105) *Ruff trade:* **Alan Rickman** *and* **Anna Calder Marshall** *with Birmingham Rep's* **The Devil is an Ass** *in 1976.*

ALL THE WORLD'S OUR STAGE

(106) *Opposite above and* (107) *left: Schiller's*
**Mary Stuart, 1958.**
(108) *Top: Teatro Piccolo with Goldoni's*
**Servant of Two Masters, 1956.**
(109) *Bottom:* **Diana Wynward** *in* **A Winter's Tale** *in*
*Peter Brook's* **1951** *production.*

*(110) Above: Taking no chances!* **Peter Ustinov**
*adapted Mussorgsky's incomplete opera of Gogol's*
**The Marriage** *in 1982, directed it, and starred in it.*
*(111) Opposite:* **John Gielgud** *as Leontes in*
**The Winter's Tale, 1951**.

*chapter three*

ALL THE WORLD'S OUR STAGE

*(112) Above right: **John Kani** in a powerful production of **Miss Julie, 1985**. (113) Above and (114) right: Market Theatre's **Born in the RSA, 1986**.*

*(115) Playwright **Athol Fugard** rehearses **Dimetes** in **1975** with **Yvonne Bryceland**.*

*Warning: Edinburgh's Festivals can seriously damage your health!*
*(116) A centurion takes a tobacco break from Peter Stein's*
**Julius Caesar, 1993.**

*(117) Festival director* **Peter Diamand** *in typical pose,* **1973***.*

*(118) The ever inventive **Wooster Group** in 1986.*

*(119) National Theatre of Craiova's* **Ubu Rex** *brought*
*the old Empire briefly to life in* **1991** *before its rebirth*
*as the Festival Theatre in* **1994.**

*(120) Above left: The Gate Theatre, Dublin's* **Salome** *in* **1989**.

*(121) Below left: Peter Stein's epic* **Julius Caesar** *at the Royal Highland Exhibition Hall in* **1993**. *Unscheduled noises off were provided by British Airways.*

*(122) Above:* **Blood Wedding** *staged in* **1986** *with* **Yerma** *to commemorate the 50th anniversary of the death of Federico Garcia Lorca.*

*(123) The English Stage Company with John Osborne's*
**Luther** *starring* **Albert Finney** *in 1961.*

*(124)* **Hywel Bennett** *as* **Long John Silver** *in the 1990*
**Treasure Island**. *The cast hired and fired 6 parrots before*
*they found a properly attentive winged thespian!*

*(125) Bristol Old Vic,* **Troilus** *and* **Cressida** *in 1979. Oh yes it is!*

*(126) Above: Glasgow invades Edinburgh. The Citizens' Theatre Company
with **Don Carlos** in 1995.*

*Opposite: (127) top, **Frank McGuinness's** powerful **Observe the Sons
of Ulster Marching Towards the Somme**, Abbey Theatre, Dublin, 1995.*

*(128) bottom left, **Luc Bondy's** inventive **The Hour We Knew Nothing
Of Each Other**, Schaubühne Theater, Berlin, 1994.*

*(129) bottom right, TAG Theatre with **Lewis Grassic Gibbon's** trilogy
**A Scots Quair** in 1993.*

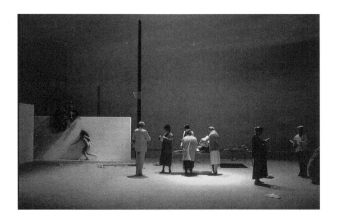

———◆———

(130) *Above: Since his arrival in* **1992 Brian McMaster** *has lured the major directorial talents to Edinburgh.*
*Opposite: (131) top left, A man for all art forms, the engaging*
**Peter Sellars**; *(132) top right,* **Patrice Chéreau** *directed* **Dans La Solitude des Champs de Coton** *in which he also starred in* **1995**,
*(133) bottom left:* **Peter Stein** *and (134) bottom right,* **Luc Bondy**.

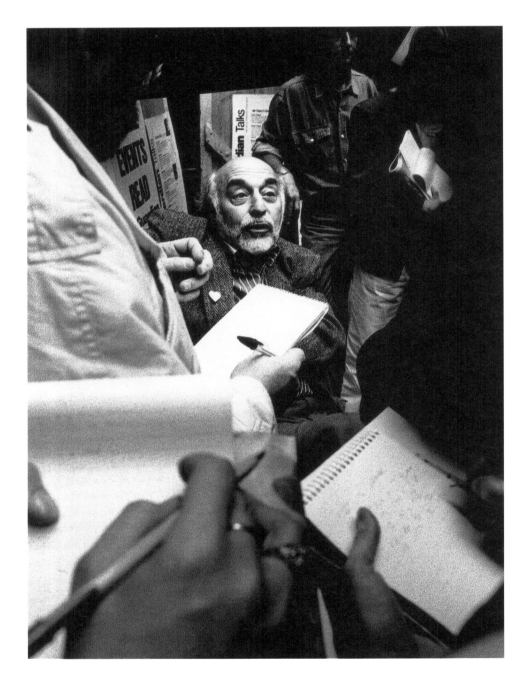

*(135)* **Frank Dunlop** *stages an inpromptu cabaret for the press in the courtyard of the Old Traverse Theatre,* ***1991.***

*(136) **Tadeusz Kantor** in Edinburgh with **Cricot 2** in 1980.*

*The Festival has staged intermittent literary conferences since*
*the early 60s attracting a glittering cast.*
*Opposite: (137) top left **Naomi Mitchison**, (138) top right **Henry Miller**,*
*(139) bottom left **Muriel Spark** and (140) bottom right **Angus Wilson**.*
*(141) Above: **Samuel Beckett**.*

*(142)* **Dylan Thomas** *talks to the nation via the Corporation.*

*Above, clockwise from top left:*
*(143)* **James Baldwin**,
*(144)* **W.H. Auden**,
*(145)* **Jean Paul Sartre**,
*and (146) with* **John Drummond –**
**Peter Schaeffer**,
**Peter Hall** *and* **Michael Frayn**.

# *Strolling* Players

Archery contests, hot air ballooning, sports days and garden parties. More country dancing than you could shake a sporran at. You would be amazed m'dears at the events with which the citizenry chose to garland its shiny new summer toy.

But the jewel in the social crown was the Festival Club. In its heyday a place where the stars could glitter by night outshone only occasionally by the Assembly Rooms' chandeliers in George Street. By day one could take tea and scones or that new-fangled coffee. By night it was cocktails, best frocks, and supper only ten tables away from real live performing persons.

The Festival Club was then an institution; a place to see and be seen. Currently its former premises are home to one of the Fringe's largest venues, and it has fallen on decidedly less glamourous times in the University Staff Club.

But the new Festival home in the Lawnmarket heralds the dawn of another new club, though probably not a return to obligatory hats and tweeds.

Other hallowed social traditions include the Lord Provost's party, a bash which has seen such implausible sights as Mark Morris giving the Dashing White Sergeant big licks, and where, years before, gold lamé flared catsuits were *de rigueur*. And that was only the men.

But less official parties abound. The Edinburgh Festival, in the nicest possible way, is something of a three week endurance test. Still, there are some 11 drabber months in which to effect a convalescence.

*Previous pages: (147) Swapping gossip at the club.*
*1972 was a good year for millinery and taxidermy.*
*(148) Daytime heydays circa 1954.*

*(149) Above: Non calorie-controlled strings.*
***The Viennese Café** in **1983** with an impromptu*
***Leonard Friedman** trio.*

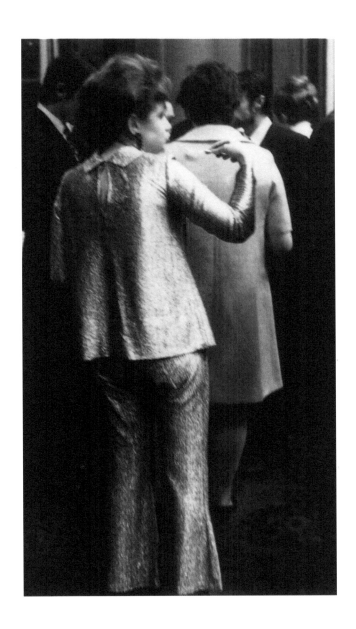

*(150) Gold lamé flares - de rigueur at civic receptions*
***c.1967.***

*(151)* **Burt Lancaster** *takes tea with the Festival in*
***1976.*** *The shades proved an unnecessary accessory.*

*(152) Opposite top: Transatlantic nobility - **Douglas Fairbanks Jnr** meets the **Earl of Dalkeith.***

*(153) Opposite bottom: **The Bings** with pet dachshund.*

*(154) Above: **Princess Grace** arrives for the **1976** Festival.*

*(155) Above right: **Lord Harewood** with (l to r) **Galina Vishnevskaya, Dmitri Shostakovitch** and **Mstislav Rostropovitch, 1962.***

*(156) Below right: **André Previn** discusses where to find a barber, **1973**.*

*(157) Even Lord Provosts get twitchy waiting for their guests, 1948.*

*(158) Opposite: The embryonic Festival Fringe - no cowboys,*
*just the odd archer.*

*(159 & 160) Country dancing and partying in posh gardens - de rigueur in certain circles.*

*(161) Above: "Lord" Provost **Eleanor McLaughlin** becomes an instant fan of **Lenny Henry** in 1988.*

*(162) The inaugural Festival Council lays its ambitious plans in 1947.*

*(163) Top:* **Barenboim, Bernstein, du Pré**
*and friends share a festival sofa in* **1973.**
*(164) Above:* **Robert Ponsonby** *congratulates*
**Maria Callas** *after her performance, 1957.*

*(165) Above: **Mark Morris** and **Peter Sellars** - performers and Festival groupies, **1995**.*

*(166) Above right: **Rudolf Nureyev** on his trolley at Edinburgh Airport, **1984**.*

*(167) Right: **Günter Wand** arrives in **1994** for his concert with the **NDR Symphony Orchestra**.*

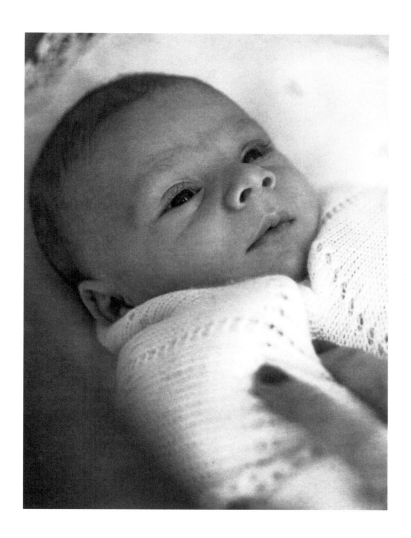

*(168)* **Gerard**, *son of* **Yehudi Menuhin**, *born during the*
**1948** *Festival.*

# Life *on the* High C's

Edinburgh was one fledgling festival which didn't have to worry where its next opera was coming from. Founding director Rudolf Bing was General Manager of Glyndebourne, and that company was the operatic bulwark of the early years.

They opened with *The Marriage of Figaro* and, in a nod to their new location, Verdi's *Macbeth.* By 1950 Beecham was part of the regular proceedings – and you don't get many conductors who feature in both the Verdi Requiem and an open air concert on the castle esplanade with massed military bands. The Lady Beecham, clearly possessing either a nervous disposition or a well developed sense of the ridiculous, decreed that her husband would front the latter proceedings clad in a tin hat. Unfazed, new Festival director Ian Hunter duly filled in army requisition form number 108 and collected the necessary from the Quartermaster's Stores.

That last extravaganza also had a fireworks display, the forerunner of the Fireworks Concert which now brings a quarter of a million people on to Princes Street each year.

The foreign contingent was led by Hamburg State Opera in 1952, a company in remarkably fine shape post-war considering what that city and that country had to deal with. Fittingly they opened with Beethoven's *Fidelio* that year, in a six opera season, coming back in 1956 with *Oedipus Rex* and *Salome* and again in 1968 with an even more ambitious triple bill of *The Flying Dutchman, Elektra,* and *Ariadne auf Naxos.*

La Piccola Scala from Milan, unsurprisingly, majored on Italian works. The audience in 1957 was duly appreciative of a diet of Rossini and Donizetti, but they went into collective ecstasy over Bellini's *La Sonnambula* – which may just have had something to do with the soprano cast as Amina. The critics had the odd pompous sideswipe at Maria Callas, the paying customers uniformly adored her.

The following year also gave Edinburgh the chance to hear another of the finest voices of that era, as Victoria de Los Angeles arrived for *La Vida Breve.*

(169) Previous page: **Maria Callas** *as* **Amina** *in* **La**
**Sonnambula** *in 1957.*

(170) *Above: Founding director* **Rudolf Bing**.

(171) *Opposite: He's boyish, he's slender, he's* **Pavarotti**!

It wasn't until the 60s that the Royal Opera Covent
Garden managed to cross the border, but with them
came Joan Sutherland as Lucia di Lammermoor, and
Britten and Pears' *A Midsummer Night's Dream.*

The sixties brought a welcome influx from
Eastern Europe too, with Budapest's Bartok
programme in '63 followed by Prague's homage to
Janáçek the following year, and The Bavarian State
Opera the year after that, with the first UK
performance of Strauss' *Intermezzo.*

But in 1967 a rather younger company made its
much heralded appearance at the Festival. Launched
just four years before, Scottish Opera was the
realisation of a long held dream of SNO's Alexander
Gibson. That first year they married *The Rake's*
*Progress* at the King's to a performance of *The Soldier's*
*Tale* at the Assembly Hall. And so began a long and
rich association including many performances about
which incurable Festival fans still warmly reminisce.

Janet Baker joined the cast of their *Trojans* in
1972, for instance, a six hour epic. They don't make
audiences like that any more.

It was '67 too which helped cement Edinburgh
Festival Opera's growing talent as starspotters. Joan
Sutherland was the main event in Haydn's *Orfeo ed*
*Euridice*, but there was also Bellini's *I Capuletti ed i*
*Montecchi*, conducted by Abbado. And, as the
programme coyly noted, among those the cast would
include was a slim young tenor, name of Pavarotti.

Tito Gobbi came with Florence's Teatro Communale in 1969 as both producer and soloist and the Italian connection was further cemented in '71 when Edinburgh Festival Opera collaborated with Maggio Musicale Fiorentino in a production of Rossini's *La Cenerentola* which featured the LSO conducted by Claudio Abbado, Teresa Berganza as Angelica and the Scottish Opera Chorus. That's what you can safely call international.

That same year the greatly acclaimed Deutsche Oper Berlin were also in Edinburgh, and Deutsche Oper am Rhein came in '72 with a much praised production of *Die Soldaten*.

But in '73, with Scottish Opera on tour in London, Festival director Peter Diamand decided it was time for Edinburgh Festival Opera to spread its wings. And nobody could accuse them of thinking small with Peter Ustinov the producer of a *Don Giovanni* conducted by Daniel Barenboim with Geraint Evans and Heather Harper. It was a fairly high risk strategy given the international companies who could have been brought in to plug any programming gap, but Diamand saw it as part of his firm policy of encouraging indigenous enterprise, and, in the event, he was handsomely rewarded for his courage.

Some of these partnerships were renewed two years later when Evans produced a *Marriage of Figaro* with Barenboim at the helm of the English Chamber Orchestra and was joined by Teresa Berganza, Dietrich Fischer-Dieskau and Heather Harper. It had another outing the following year as the Festival celebrated its thirtieth year.

But it was 1977 which really set the Festival's opera programme alight. Edinburgh Festival Opera this time had set its sights on *Carmen* and was not about to spare any expense. Teresa Berganza was persuaded to make her debut in the title role opposite Placido Domingo.

The press went collectively loopy, interviewing anything that moved and stoking up controversy about the highest ever ticket prices. In the event the £20 top price was changing hands at many times that on the black market and the production was sold out almost as soon as the tickets were printed. Cheap at twice the price was the general verdict.

Opera companies were also becoming more adventurous about going outside the charmed circle for input. Prospect Theatre's Toby Robertson was the producer and Bill Bryden the librettist for the Scottish Opera production of Robin Orr's *Hermiston* while Jonathan Miller produced Kent's *Traviata*.

The Germans continued their love affair with Edinburgh throughout the eighties. Cologne Opera came twice, and Dresden and Hamburg both visited. Welsh National Opera also made their debut with *Tamburlaine* in '82 – produced and designed by Philip Prowse, one of the triumvirate (with Giles Havergal and Robert David MacDonald) responsible for the high regard in which the Glasgow Citizens' Theatre is now held.

Yet perhaps the dominant event in that decade was provided by Americans. Washington Opera had already visited in '84 with their idiosyncratic choice of a Gian Carlo Menotti double bill: *The Telephone* and *The Medium*.

But it was Houston Grand Opera who pulled off the major *coup de théâtre* four years later with their

*(172)* **Nixon in China** *directed by* **Peter Sellars** *in* **1988**.
*The cast were eerily like the originals.*
*(173) Opposite:* **Joan Sutherland** *as* **Lucia di Lammermoor**
*with the Royal Opera, Covent Garden in* **1961**.

astonishing *Nixon in China*. John Adam's minimalist score sharply divided opinions, but Alice Goodman's libretto and particularly Peter Sellars' direction made *Nixon* an extraordinary event. Some of the most persistent memories are visual - a cast looking alarmingly like their real life characters and the arrival on stage of an equally lifelike passenger jet.

Of course opera need not be grand. If you needed any proof you went in the eighties to Leith Theatre to be entertained by a company rejoicing in the title of Folkopera of Stockholm. The purists sniffed as they romped through *The Magic Flute*, gave a new meaning to small scale with *Aida* and played *Turandot* with a 16 piece-band.

*(174)* ***Bluebeard's Castle*** *− one of the double bill with Canadian Opera Company directed by **Robert Lepage** in 1993.*

But as a way of bringing in a new opera audience and forging a rapport with them the Swedes did the Festival no harm at all.

At the more controversial end of the scale came the world premiere of Mark Anthony Turnage's *Greek* directed by Steven Berkoff, one of an increasing number of productions across the arts which chose Edinburgh as a prestigious launch pad.

The visit of Leningrad's Maly Theatre with *Queen of Spades* in 1986 − when joiners had to saw up the set to make it fit the restrictions imposed by the small and not so perfectly formed King's Theatre − emphasised what the world and its Festival-going neighbour had long since concluded: Edinburgh would never be the complete Festival City without a proper home for major opera and ballet companies.

In fact over four decades some six opera house schemes had been proposed − some of them prestigious, others frankly impractical.

But for much of the debate it was accepted that the site would be a conveniently large city-owned piece of ground in Castle Terrace. And for much of the debate a hole in the ground is exactly what it remained, outside of those years when more entrepreneurial spirits constructed a tent there in August to create a temporary venue.

Finally the site was sold to a developer who put up a modern, though aesthetically pleasing office block in the bowels of which is a splendid new theatre for the Traverse.

*(175) Worth the 40 year wait -* ***Edinburgh's Festival Theatre*** *has a new facade on the lovingly remodelled Empire auditorium.*

(176) *Glyndebourne's* **Don Giovanni**, **Paolo Silveri**, *has his moustache artificially enhanced in* **1948**.

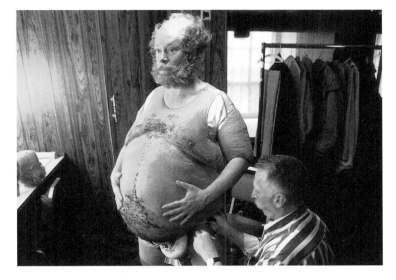

(177) **Donald Maxwell** *has the stuffing knocked into him for the* **WNO Falstaff, 1993**.

For a while it seemed a deal might be done with the owners of the Playhouse. But finally, with one last heave from the local authorities and the local enterprise company, and some determined support from the business community it was agreed that the old Empire would be rescued from the "legs eleven" lobby and restored to its former glory. Added to the original auditorium with its fine acoustic and excellent sight lines would be an enlarged stage, new fly tower, retractable pit and those essentials of modern performing arts – suitable quarters for the sponsoring classes.

While that project got underway, with not a few financial hiccups, the Bolshoi Opera came two years running and the young Scottish composer James MacMillan was given the accolade of a retrospective

of his work including the emotionally charged mixed media *Visitatio Sepulchri* – the orchestration, singing, and choreography vying for the attention of the audience. The custom of honouring talent before it is six feet under is greatly to be encouraged.

That same year highlighted the apparently endless inventiveness of theatre director Robert Lepage who masterminded the Canadian Opera Company double bill of *Bluebeard's Castle* (with Jane Gilbert) and *Erwartung* (Rebecca Blankenship) to a rapturous reception at the Playhouse.

A similar marriage of theatrical and operatic ingenuity was undertaken by Welsh National Opera with Peter Stein's *Falstaff* starring Donald Maxwell and Bryn Terfel.

*(178) Canadian Opera Company's **1993 Erwartung**.*

But at last, in 1994, opera had a home which could welcome any company in the world. And fittingly it was Scottish Opera who had the privilege of staging the first Festival production in the new Festival Theatre with *Fidelio*. The company's previous attempt at Beethoven's only opera had not been an unqualified success – the acting then of the 'stand and deliver' variety. But there was no doubting the quality of their 1994 version.

In contrast to the starkly dramatic staging of *Fidelio* came The Australian Opera's colourful and sumptuous *A Midsummer Night's Dream* which made joyous use of every yard of a stage which is now the largest and most versatile in the UK. And the Kirov enjoyed the same freedom in 1995 as they returned with *Sadko* and the *The Legend of the Invisible City of Kitezh*.

Meanwhile, along at the Lyceum, Peter Sellars continued his journey of personal exploration with *I Was Looking At The Ceiling And Then I Saw The Sky*. Some critics felt that "Ceiling Sky" with its seven episodic sections on young Los Angeles lifestyles shouldn't properly have been categorised as opera at all. But as evidence of Sellars' passionate concern for the social issues of his times, it provided one of the only rules about Festivals worth observing: don't ever be predictable.

It also provided a sales gimmick for one of Edinburgh's more venerable purveyors of reading material. "I was looking at the window and then I saw the books" ran their new poster.

*(179) **John Gielgud** produced **A Midsummmer Night's Dream** for Covent Garden Opera in **1961**.*

*(180)* **The Australian Opera** *make maximum use of the*
*Festival Theatre stage with* **A Midsummer Night's**
**Dream** *in 1994.*

(181) *Right: Scottish Opera with* **The Soldier's Tale** *in* **1967.**

(182) *Below right: Edinburgh's City Fathers dispatched a delegation to Frankfurt to determine whether or not their festival could cope with nude nuns. Apparently it could! And did!* **The Fiery Angel** *was performed at the King's in* **1970.**

(183) *Opposite: Folkopera of Stockholm's somewhat idiosyncratic* **Aida, 1986.**

*Glyndebourne was effectively the Festival's
resident opera company in the early years.*
*(184) Opposite:* ***Ariadne auf Naxos, 1950.***
*(185) Above:* ***Falstaff, 1955.***
*(186) Right:* ***Don Giovanni, 1948.***

(187) *Above: Hamburg State Opera's dramatic*
**Salome** *in 1956.*
(188) *Right: English Opera Group with*
**The Rape of Lucretia** *in 1963.*

(189) *Teutonic Overtures:*
*Above: Cologne Opera's **La Clemenza di Tito** in 1981 (left **Brigitte Fassbaender**, right, **Daphne Evangelatos**).*
(190) *Below right: Deutsche Oper Berlin with **Die Entführung aus dem Serail** in 1971.*

*(191)* **Ustinov** *and* **Barenboim** *publicise their* **Don Giovanni** *in 1974.*

*(192) Opposite:* **Valery Gergiev**, *Musical Director The Kirov Opera, 1995.*

*(193) The Kirov Opera's **Sadko**, 1995.*

*(194) Above:* **Galina Gorchakova**
*in make-up for* **Kitezh**.
*She also entranced Queen's Hall audiences
in* **1994** *and* **1995**.

*(195) Above right:* **Kirov** *dressing room.*

*(196) Right: The Kirov Opera's* **Sadko**.

*(197) Far right: The Kirov Opera's* **Kitezh**.

(198) *Above:* **I Was Looking At The Ceiling And Then I Saw The Sky, 1995.**

(199) *Left: Backstage.*

(200) *Above left:* **Robert Lepage** *had twin triumphs with Canadian Opera Company in* **1993** *with* **Bluebeard's Castle** *and* **Erwartung**.
(201) *Above middle:* **Baz Luhrmann** *director of The Australian Opera's* **A Midsummer Night's Dream, 1994**
(202) *Above right: Festival Director* **John Drummond** *escapes the shadow of John Knox.*
(203) *Left:* **1993** *and* **James MacMillan** *is given a Festival retrospective while still young, gifted and alive. A welcome innovation!*

*(204) Above: The Classic Pairing - **Berganza** and **Domingo** in the 1977 Carmen.*
*Tickets were an unprecedented £20 and sold out overnight.*

*(205) Left: **Berganza** poses with suitable backdrop as she arrives in Edinburgh for the **1975 Marriage of Figaro**.*

*(206) Above: **Berganza** embracing **Abbado**. Note the 'aide memoire' on the left forearm.*

(207) *Above: The foyer of the newly opened **Festival Theatre**, **1994**.*
(208) *Opposite: **Mark Anthony Turnage's Greek**, premiered in Edinburgh before it transferred to London in **1988**.*

# Best Seats *in the* House

*(209) We are about to be amused:* **The Queen** *and* **Prince Philip** *at the Usher Hall.*

Attention to detail is, naturally, the unfailingly observed motto of the Edinburgh International Festival.

Members of the planning staff were therefore instinctively aware in the early years that Royal personages are not constructed as other mortals.

And so it came to pass that if a Royal Patron were to express a desire for musical enlightenment at the Usher Hall, dramatic diversion at the Assembly Hall, thespian delights at the Lyceum or operatic overtures at the King's, seats were reserved accordingly. Actually not so much seats as, well, thrones.

Whole rows of standard fitments would be hastily removed to accommodate furnishings more likely to cosset the regal posterior.

Those who have survived four hour performances at the Assembly Hall in particular, where the pews are designed to remind sinners of their lowly status, can only envy crowned heads one of the more desirable Festival perks of their trade.

BEST SEATS IN THE HOUSE

(210) Top left: **1949** and **The Queen** and **Princess Margaret** attend **The Thrie Estates**.

(211) Top right: **The Queen** and **Princess Margaret** at The King's in **1950**.

(212) Bottom left: The Usher Hall rises for the national anthem.

(213) Bottom right: **The Queen Mother** and **Princess Margaret** at the Usher Hall for the Inaugural Festival in **1947**.

# Visual *Delights*

*(214) Above: An arresting **Epstein** bronze.*

*(215) Opposite: Getting the message from **David Mach**.*

The Festival had given a nod in the direction of the visual arts since year one... but nothing much more than that until Ian Hunter took over from Rudolf Bing to plan the 1950 programme.

And during his six year reign Edinburgh had a number of exhibitions of major international importance... in particular the series on Impressionist and Post Impressionist art which began with Degas in '52, swiftly followed in succeeding years by Renoir, Cézanne, Gauguin, Braque and Monet.

Yet the visual arts have had a pretty chequered Festival history so far as official programming has been concerned, from the unmissable to the frankly mundane.

However the National Galleries of Scotland, and indeed dozens of other lesser visual luminaries, have been happy to use the obvious showcase of Edinburgh in August to mount complementary exhibitions, often incorporating the cream of private collections rarely seen in the UK.

The sixties brought masterpieces from the Bührle collection in Zurich, and modern treasures from the Heine Onstad collection in Oslo; the seventies the Armand Hammer collection, and the Smithsonian was persuaded to part with some of its eclectic collection in the eighties for an exhibition which stayed for many months. By common consent the Epstein memorial exhibition in the early sixties was a triumphant success, as was the ambitious *Vienna 1900* in 1983.

John Drummond, the then director, counts that amongst the achievements of which he is still most proud, given that the exhibition was married to some 120 other Festival events from literature and lectures to the orchestral content. *Vienna 1900* celebrated his belief, he says, that "culture is one world, not a series of ghettoes".

Over the five decades nobody could accuse Edinburgh's curators and exhibition organisers of a narrow range of interest. Certainly there has been constant homage paid to the Impressionists following those early successes and the 1990 *Cézanne and Poussin: The Classical Vision of Landscape* proved another spectacular treasure trove.

But everything from German Expressionism through Belgian Surrealism, Zen, Persian miniatures, Balkan primitives and North West Coast Indian art has had its day in Edinburgh.

Neither has indigenous talent been neglected. *Painting in Scotland: The Golden Age* was staged by the

Talbot Rice in '86, the Gallery of Modern Art's *Vigorous Imagination* the following year celebrated new Scottish art and in 1989 all the National Galleries raided their collections for *Scottish Art since 1900*.

Throughout all of which photography has tended to be treated as an impoverished relation, a sin of omission which was rectified in part by 1993's *The Waking Dream*, a celebration of photography's first century.

⟡

*(216) Top: **Peter Howson** with typically potent image.*

*(217) Above: **John Bellany** gives **Ekkehard Schall** the conducted tour of his retrospective.*

*(218) Previous pages (left): **Ian Hunter,** Festival Director from **1950** to **1955**.*

*(219) right: 5 million dollars worth of **Rembrandt** arrives in Armand Hammer's private jet.*

*(220)* **Waking Dreams** *for weary foot soldiers,* **1993**.

# Those *Dancing* Years

*Now and Then. (221)* **Merce Cunningham** *as Guru,* **1994** *and (222) opposite, as Principal Dancer,* **1973** *in a classic shot by Jack Mitchell.*

For the first seven years of its life the Festival enjoyed an annual residency of the Sadler's Wells Company at a time when its principals included Margot Fonteyn and Robert Helpmann, and the Empire Theatre was still available as a venue. Not a few dance fans went into a decline when the premises fell victim to the national bingo craze. Now of course it's back in its former glory as the Festival Theatre which opened the doors of its splendid new brass and glass fronted foyer in 1994.

The contribution of the Sadler's Wells company in those years wasn't just a matter of quality performances. They sought out and encouraged upcoming choreographic talents and the Edinburgh audiences were able to enjoy new work by John Cranko and Kenneth MacMillan at the time they were just beginning to build reputations for innovation. MacMillan's *Noctambules* in 1956 caused a bit of a flurry in the critical doo'cots, but made a lasting impression on its audience.

*(223) **Edward Villella** and New York City Ballet in George Balanchine's **Apollo** in 1967.*

Although classical ballet in particular has been an integral part of the Festival for all its five decades, some of the individual years have offered feast or relative famine presumably according to the whim and artistic predelictions of assorted directors. And

successive years also brought wonderful contrasts. The start of the American invasion with American National Ballet Theatre with its refreshing irreverence and the music of Leonard Bernstein in 1950; the acclaimed *Homage to Diaghilev* in 1954 on the 25th anniversary of his death, a sentiment echoed in 1987 with Ballet Theatre Francais' *Homage Aux Ballets Russes and Diaghilev* featuring Nureyev, of whom rather more later. And the astonishing energy of the Kabuki company from Japan in '55 juxtaposed with a programme from the Royal Danish Ballet including a new production of *Romeo & Juliet*.

The American influence on Festival dance has been profound in terms of the consistent policy of most US companies to challenge the accepted order of things. Jerome Robbins' Ballet USA in 1959 provided a work totally without music – an innovation which apparently led to a particularly intense performance.

The legendary Martha Graham Dance Company brought fresh dimensions to contemporary work in 1963; George Balanchine came with New York City Ballet in 1967 and a year later the Alvin Ailey Company brought a cutting edge of political comment to their work in much the same way as Bill T. Jones was to explore 90s issues a quarter of a century later.

As ever the search for new and challenging venues exercised the minds of the organisers... sometimes at great personal risk. One Festival administrator, so enamoured of his exploratory

*(224)* ***The Four Sons of Aymon*** *– a Festival debut for Murrayfield Ice Rink in 1962.*

examination of the artistic possibilities of Murrayfield Ice Rink, contrived to fall down an open manhole whilst warming conversationally to his theme during a walkabout.

The company which benefited from his high risk strategy was the Ballet du XXe Siècle from Belgium, whose *Four Sons of Aymon* in 1962 was generally agreed to offer a total theatrical experience, and had the same mind-altering effect on its ballet audience as *Orlando Furioso* did for the theatre variety eight years later.

More predictably warm receptions too for the first appearance of the Paul Taylor Dance Company in 1966, and the sheer professionalism of Nederlands Dans Theater four years on.

Of course there were sometimes weird and often wonderful influences on dance from many less obvious parts of the choreographic globe. It would probably be churlish to suggest that the unparalleled enthusiasm of the press photographers for the national company from Senegal in 1972 in any way related to the fact that much of their work was of the topless variety.

And then there was the Mummenschanz company in '74 whose mixture of dance and mime and extraordinary costume invention defied description but enchanted every customer.

The onward march of the legends continued in '78 with the first appearance of Pina Bausch's Wuppertal Dance Theatre. Bausch has left indelible imprints on the Festival programme and indelible imprints too on the memories of those whose task it is to perform the more menial chores required to put genius on stage.

Thus was one of the stranger backstage sights; the prospect, in 1995, of an assortment of husky stage hands doggedly fashioning many thousands of pink paper carnations for the production of *Nelken*. They also serve who only sit and sew.

1979 was the debut year for the Merce Cunningham Company who supplemented their official programme with eagerly awaited workshops from the master and his young company. A year later brought a new company to the Festival scene...

(225) *1991 and one of the nicer surprises – the unique talents of* **Mummenschanz**.

(226) *The Amalgamated Union of Carnation Operatives prepare for the* **Pina Bausch Nelken** *in 1995*.

except that it was also a familiar one. Elizabeth West had originally visited with Western Theatre Ballet in 1961. After she died, the company formed the nucleus of the first Scottish Ballet company under Peter Darrell. By coincidence that first bill included the world premiere of *Cheri*, created for guest star Galina Samsova. Ms. Samsova is currently the artistic director of Scottish Ballet.

More American contrasts in the early eighties, with both San Francisco Ballet and the Dan Wagoner Dancers featuring in a 1981 programme which also brought London Contemporary Dance Theatre north.

And as the Festival moved into the eighties, the dance programme moved into a different gear; not abandoning the classics but offering showcases to

those pushing at the frontiers. Sankai Juku came with their mesmeric street performances, Ballet Rambert - oddly making their very first appearance in 1983 with Merce Cunningham's *Fielding Six*, and Michael Clark, still young enough to warrant an "enfant" before the "terrible", back in his native Scotland with his company in both '85 and '88.

The 1980s also saw much of Rudolf Nureyev. He came with his Paris Opera Ballet in 1984, returned as a guest with Scottish Ballet a year later, joined the National Ballet of Canada's Diaghilev programme in '87 and returned with the Cleveland San José Ballet company in 1990. Unkinder critics suggested that by those latter years he was hardly the supple enchanter of earlier times. But there's little doubt that the

audiences felt he could still sprinkle star quality glitter over any proceedings he chose regardless of the technical merits of the performance. Still, even great big stars are entitled to a little help from their friends. *In L' Après Midi d'un Faun*, he was scheduled to leap athletically through an open window. His athleticism was usually enhanced by a shove from a couple of burly chaps backstage. Imagine then the alarm of Nureyev's stand-in when somebody forgot to advise the muscular arms that the understudy didn't need a heave. It is reported that he managed to land without entirely disappearing into the wings opposite.

    The 80s also brought us Lyon Opera Ballet, Komische Oper Ballet from Berlin, Matsuyama Ballet from Japan, Houston Ballet, Spanish National Ballet

*Is it a bird? Is it a plane?*
*(227) Above left: How do they do that?* **Changement de Pieds** *- one of 12 Ballets commissioned for the Festival in* **1958**.
*(228) Above right:* **Dan Wagoner** *with the Paul Taylor Company,* **1966**.

and the Royal Thai Ballet. While London Festival Ballet proved their versatility in a programme which both premiered the *Petrouchka Variations* and tackled Michael Clark's *Drop Your Pearls and Hog It, Girl*. It also brought us yet another variation on the well worked theme of *Macbeth*. Johann Kresnik's piece was choreographed for the Bremer Theater Company and owed rather more to sado-masochism than Shakespeare.

It also owed a sartorial debt to Sid Vicious, godfather of punk. If we note too that the amount of "blood" spilled nightly required a protective tarpaulin to be laid over the orchestra pit, you will readily imagine that this performance was not adored at first sight by the denizens of Jenner's tearoom – purveyor of scones and comfort to the gentler folk. A similar preoccupation with gore afflicted Canada's La La La Human Steps in '91, though if you like your dance accompanied by heavy metal music and heavy metal chain saws this was the gig for you. Oddly, the same year that La La La were producing the Ooooh, Aaargh's at the Playhouse, Berlin Ballet produced shocks of a different kind just two weeks later. Their ambitious *Ring Round the Ring*, Maurice Bejart's four hour adaptation of Wagner's Ring Cycle might have produced controversy, but it was a truly stunning spectacle.

Different yet again, and bringing his customary air of surrealism to that year's proceedings with *Desirs Parade*, was the ever inventive Philippe Genty who had made a huge impression the year before with *Derives*.

The nineties brought, above all, the best of contemporary American dance. It brought too some splendid cross fertilisation between the art forms.

*(229)* The sensational **Ring Around The Ring** from *Berlin Ballet in* **1991**.
*(230) Opposite:* **Mark Morris** *and* **Yo-Yo Ma**, **1995**.

The Lucinda Childs Dance Company celebrated its 20th birthday with an Edinburgh debut in 1994, with music from Philip Glass. Glass's music often provided their inspiration just as they've gained from collaboration with director Robert Wilson.

The Bill T. Jones/Arnie Zane Dance Company arrived with a huge reputation and a very definitive agenda. Some critics find Jones' mix of dance and polemic inappropriate. Others consider that he has given contemporary dance an important voice in contemporary politics. Nobody could deny the power of his work; not least those routines based on personal bereavement and dealing with AIDS.

Bill T. Jones also provided the Festival with one of its more unusual customer complaints. In its courteous way, the Festival programme compilers had advised the audience that the piece in question contained nudity. In the event, it didn't. And one woman berated marketing director Joanna Baker on the grounds that the performance was not as advertised and, indeed, probably contravened the Trades Descriptions Act. So no nudes are not necessarily good news.

But if the last few years of the Edinburgh Festival's dance programme have belonged to any one performer it is surely Mark Morris. A perfectionist for whom the music is as important as the choreography, his appearances have provided a richness of musical experience to match the incredible quality of his work. That he is a towering talent goes without saying. But his value lies too in his profound distaste for pretentiousness and elitism. Mark Morris has not just been about thrilling performances on the stages of Edinburgh – or, bizzarely, following a fire in the Playhouse, the Meadowbank Sports Centre. Schoolchildren and pensioners and all manner of locals have fallen under his considerable spell in education initiatives run by the Festival with Lothian Regional Council.

His style was nowhere more apparent than the performance of *The Hard Nut* in 1995 which followed Miami City Ballet's more conventional *Nutcracker*. Seeing them in that order was fascinating. Seeing them in the reverse would have done no favours to the visitors from Florida.

Such is his enthusiasm for the arts in general that it's not unusual to see Morris with fellow Festival groupies like Peter Sellars catching late night shows after their own, and attending others on their nights off. In 1995 the Film Festival premiered a production which followed the progress of cellist Yo-Yo Ma collaborating with Morris in a dance version of one of Bach's cello suites. The film was shot through with mutual respect, much humour, and utter dedication. You can't demand much more.

*Dancers need hands!*

*(231) Above: **Ram Gopal, 1956**.*

*(232) Opposite: **Martha Graham, 1963**.*

*(233 & 234)* **The Hard Nut**, *before and after:*
**The Mark Morris Dance Group, 1995.**

*(235) The much photographed Ensemble National du Senegal, **1972**.*

*(236) Left: The incomparable **Fonteyn** in **La Peri** with the Royal Ballet in **1960**.*

*(237) Above: **Swan Lake** with Sadler's Wells in **1956**.*

*(238) Opposite: **The Firebird** with Sadler's Wells in **1954**.*

*(239)* **Bill T. Jones** *tells it like it is in* **1993**.

*(240)* **Nureyev** *– degree of difficulty 5.9! Prodigal Son,* **1975***.*

*(241)* **Clive Thompson** *defies gravity on behalf of the Martha Graham Dance Company,* **1963***.*

*(242) London Contemporary Dance Company,* **Dances of Love and Death, 1981.**

(243) Top left: Pina Bausch's
**Nelken, 1995**.

(244) Top right: Mark Morris Dance
Group, **Dido and Aeneas, 1992**.

(245) Bottom left: **La Vita –**
Jean Pierre Perreault, **1994**.

(246) Bottom right: American Indian
Dance Theatre, **1990**.

*chapter eight*

THOSE DANCING YEARS

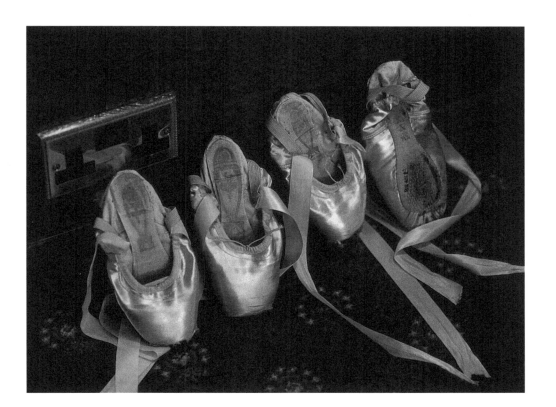

(247) Top left: *Essential tools of the trade.*
(248) Top right: ***Miami City Ballet***.
(249) Bottom left: *Final touches to* ***Nutcracker*** *make-up.*
(250) Bottom right: ***Pina Bausch*** *and friends,* ***1995***.

(251) *Left:* **Edward Villella**, *1994.*

(252) *Top:* **Pina Bausch**, *1995.*

(253) *Above: Mark Morris Dance Group*
*Schools Project* **1995.**

(254) *Opposite:* **George Balanchine**
*with feathered fan,* **1952.**

*(255)* **Twyla Tharp** *brought her New York based company to Edinburgh in* **1976.**

(256) Top left: **The Bill T. Jones/Arnie Zane Dance Company** *in* **1995**.

(257) Top right: *Not ballet as we knew it, captain.* **La La La Human Steps** *at the Playhouse with* **Infante** *in* **1991**.

(258) Bottom left: **Sankai Juku** *take their show on the road,* **1982**.

*(259) Above and (260) opposite:* **L' Allegro**, **Il Penserosa ed
Il Moderato**, *Mark Morris Dance Group,* **1994.**

# chapter eight

---✦---

## CREDIT WHERE IT'S DUE

We are grateful to the following photographers for permission to use their material in this volume:

Paul Shillabeer's daughter, Mrs Pauline Grierson 1, 15, 16, 17, 20, 27, 29, 34, 37, 48, 49, 52, 53, 57, 58, 64, 67, 74, 76, 79, 82, 83, 85, 88, 91, 92, 95, 96, 97, 98, 103, 104, 106, 107, 108, 109, 111, 123, 137, 138, 139, 140, 145, 150, 152, 155, 156, 157, 158, 159, 160, 162, 168, 170, 176, 179, 181, 182, 184, 185, 186, 187, 188, 209, 210, 211, 212, 213, 218, 224, 228, 231, 235, 236, 237, 238.

Clive Barda
Performing Arts Library
52 Agate Road
London W6 0AH.
Telephone 0181 748 2002:
4, 8, 9, 12, 13, 14, 21, 22, 23, 24, 25, 33, 40, 41, 42, 43, 44, 45, 46, 47, 116, 126, 130, 131, 132, 133, 134, 165, 167, 175, 177, 180, 191, 192, 194, 195, 199, 200, 201, 206, 207, 220, 226, 230, 233, 234, 243, 245, 247, 248, 249, 250, 251, 252, 253, 259, 260.

Sean Hudson
92 Montgomery Street
Edinburgh EH7 5HE.
Telephone 0131 556 8966:
39, 60, 61, 62, 65, 75, 78, 102, 114, 119, 120, 121, 122, 124, 127, 128, 129, 174, 178, 197, 198, 203, 208, 217, 221, 229, 256, 257.

Alex "Tug" Wilson:
3, 35, 36, 55, 56, 59, 69, 81, 100, 112, 151, 166, 189, 219, 239, 242.

Bob Anderson, Glasgow: 19.

Emily Booth/PAL: 10.

Jim Caldwell/Houston Grand Opera: 172.

Donald Cooper: 73.

Ruphin Coudyzer, Johannesberg: 113.

Anthony Crickmay, The Theatre Museum, V&A: 240.

Harry Croner: 190.

Mary Gearhart: 118.

Norward Inglis: 6.

Robbie Jack: 135, 161, 225.

Kenneth Johnson: 232.

David Kingston/Studio 16: 147, 148.

Ivan Kyncl: 63.

Lennart J: Sen-Carlen: 54

Gjon Mili/Life Magazine
(© Time Warner, Inc): 255.

Jack Mitchell: 222, 227.

Don Perdue: 246.

Roger Perry: 117.

Michael Peto: 66.

Danielle Pierre: 244.

Houston Rogers/The Theatre Museum, V&A: 173.

Sefton Samuels, Manchester: 18.

Paul Schraub, Santa Cruz: 51

Eric Thorburn, The Glasgow Picture Library: 2

Überlinger/Bodensee, Germany: 32.

While every effort has been made to trace photographers and copyright holders, in some instances this has not been possible. We would like to record our thanks for the use of the following images: 7, 26, 31, 72, 84, 86, 87, 94, 99, 105, 110, 115, 125, 136, 141, 146, 149, 154, 193, 196, 202, 204, 205, 214, 215, 216, 258.

We are grateful to the following organisations for the use of copyright images:

Bremer Theater Bremen: 80

Herbert H. Breslin Inc: 171

Chicago Symphony Orchestra: 30.

Folkoperan of Stockholm: 183

The Herald, Glasgow: 101.

Hurok Attractions/ICM: 11.

Keystone Press Agency: 153.

New York City Ballet: Apollo, choreography by George Balanchine © The George Balanchine Trust. Balanchine is a trademark of The George Balanchine Trust: 223, 254.

Ninagawa Company: 77.

The Old Vic: 90.

The Open Theatre of Belgrade: 38.

Scottish Tourist Board: 5, 28, 50, 68, 70, 71, 89, 93, 142, 143, 144, 241.*

Sony Classical: 163.

Teatro alla Scala, Milan: 164, 169.

Calman cartoons © S & C Calman. Mel Calman was a regular visitor to the Festival, giving his own particular view of events in The Times and The Scotsman. We are grateful for permission to reproduce some of his cartoons in this book.

* John Atkinson was staff photographer for the Scottish Tourist Board 1947 - 1953.